SIBERIAN HUSKY DESCRIPTION

The Siberian Husky is a medium-size working dog. characteristic gait is free and effortless, with great pulling strength. Pound for pound, he the toughest draft dog in existence. It is as natural for the Siberian to work in a team of sled dogs as it is for a Pointer to point birds or a Beagle to run rabbits.

The Siberian Husky has a moderately compact body. His coat is soft and smooth, with a downy, dense undercoat. It is of medium length, but the general outline of the dog is clear-cut, without shagginess. A mature male dog should weigh between 45 and 60 pounds, and a female between 35 and 50. Height for a male should be between 21 and 23^1/$_2$ inches; for a female, the height should be between 20 and 22 inches. The Siberian Husky's tail, shaped like a neat, furry brush, is

a curve when ...ning or standing at ...it trails out behind ...ne is working or resting. When carried up, the tail does not snap flat to the back or curl to either side.

There is a wide range of color combinations in the Siberian, including solid white. The common colors are silver gray, black, copper or tan, all with white underparts, white points, and with a variety of striking mask-like markings on the head and face.

The eyes may be brown or blue. Blue eyes are characteristic and not considered "watch eyes." They are as normal as blue eyes in a human being. The Siberian Husky is one of the very few breeds recognized by the American Kennel Club in which blue eyes are desirable. Many Siberians have one brown and one blue eye, which in no way detracts from the value of the dog.

The black markings around the eyes, up the forehead and around the nose and ears of the Siberian Husky are characteristic of this intriguing breed.

CHARACTER OF THE SIBERIAN HUSKY

Although he is best known as a working and racing dog, the Siberian has proved himself to be singularly adaptable as a house pet. Being friendly and responsive to his owner and members of his family and friends, he is readily at home in an apartment or house. He seldom barks unless trained to do so. By instinct, he is non-aggressive, but he will give an excellent account of himself if attacked. He makes an efficient watch dog, mainly because his size and appearance are intimidating to anyone unacquainted with the breed. He is gentle and affectionate with clean habits, modest eating demands, and no doggy odor; in spite of his dense coat, he needs little grooming and no trimming. He adjusts well to warmer climates and indoor living.

Two puppies are better than one! When selecting your pup do not be alarmed if you cannot choose one—two do perfectly well together.

HISTORY OF THE HUSKY

As its name implies, the Siberian Husky originated in Siberia. The breed is believed to have been developed by the Chuchis, or Chukchis, an Eskimo-like people who settled in the Kolyma River Basin in northern Siberia. The combination of the tribe's isolation and the intelligent breeding system employed by its people resulted in continued improvement of the breed—and in a strain which has remained pure for over 2,000 years.

Unlike the Eskimos who migrated eastward across Alaska and Canada to Greenland and who left their dogs very much to themselves when not actually in use, the Chukchis used their dogs not only as their sole means of transportation but also as guards for their possessions and companions for their children. The dogs were treated as family pets and often shared their

The Husky developed in Siberia, one of the coldest climates on earth. Do not take pity on him and bring him in for a cold night. Doing so, and then turning him out the next night can cause serious health problems.

masters' dwellings. This does much to explain why the Siberian is noted for his tractability, gentleness, and versatility.

THE SIBERIAN HUSKY IN ALASKA

The first selected teams of Siberians in Alaska arrived shortly after 1900. They were trained and entered in the All-Alaska Sweepstakes, a non-stop race from Nome to Candle and back, a distance of 408 miles. Competing against the best racing teams in Alaska, one team set a record for the course of a little more than 74 hours.

This great race was held for ten years. In 1915, 1916, and 1917, it was won by a team of Siberians driven by Leonhard Seppala, who is acknowledged to be the greatest dogdriver of them all. For many years there was a 25-mile marathon race in Nome known as the Borden Cup Race. Seppala again set the record for this race with a time of one hour, 50 minutes and 25 seconds.

When Nome was stricken by a diphtheria epidemic in late January, 1925, the nearest serum was at Anchorage. It could be shipped north to Nenana by the Alaska Railroad, which operated all winter. But from there it would have to go 658 miles by dog team along the Tanana and Yukon Rivers, through a pass to Unalakleet, and around an arm of the Bering Sea to Nome. The serum was rushed from Nenana by relay teams, and Seppala, with 20 dogs, started from Nome to meet the relay team carrying

Because of his stamina and sustained power over long distances there is probably no better breed for racing or pulling than the Siberian Husky.

the serum. Twelve of the dogs were left to be cared for by Eskimos along the way for replacements on the return trip. Seppala drove a distance of 169 miles from Nome before he intercepted the last of the 15 relay teams which had brought the serum from Nenana.

He had already travelled 42 miles that day in a howling blizzard, with the temperature 30 degrees below zero, but he turned around and retraced the same distance—a staggering total of 84 miles in a single day under the worst possible conditions.

Although it was Seppala with his great lead dog Togo who drove the longest distance in this historic run, it was Gunnar Kasson who took the serum the last lap into Nome —and his leader, Balto, won the acclaim. Balto's statue stands in New York City's Central Park; the inscription is a tribute to all sled dogs. It reads, *"Dedicated to the indomitable spirit of the sled dogs that relayed anti-toxin 600 miles over rough ice, across treacherous waters, through Arctic blizzards, from Nenana to the relief of stricken Nome."*

Puppies, whether bred as sled dogs or companions, require both socialization and training.

Open country is the best place to practice a team of Huskies. In populated areas the distractions have a tendency to divert the dogs' concentration.

SERVICE TO MANKIND

The Siberian Husky has also been of service to mankind on Polar expeditions, having been used on the three Byrd Expeditions to the South Pole and on the Navy's Operation Deep Freeze to Antarctica.

During World War II, Siberian teams were used in search-and-rescue operations. Dogs, sleds, equipment, and driver were parachuted to downed planes to bring out casualties. Teams were also used at weather stations in Greenland and Baffin Island. At the Battle of the Bulge, Siberians helped to bring out the wounded.

"Dogs for Defense" tried to train a few for guard and attack work, but the Siberian's friendly temperament did not adapt him to this type of work. The breed's versatility in other areas is demonstrated by the fact that there are several Siberians serving as guide dogs for the blind.

STANDARD OF THE BREED

A breed standard is the criterion by which the appearance (and to a certain extent, the temperament as well) of any given dog is made subject to objective measurement. Basically the standard for any breed is a definition of the perfect dog, to which all specimens of the breed are compared. The degree of excellence of the appearance of a given dog is in direct proportion to how well that dog meets the requirements for its breed. Of course, a certain amount of subjective evaluation is involved because of the wording of the standard itself and because of factors introduced through the completely human judging apparatus.

Siberian Huskies possess a keen but friendly expression.

Even the most perfect specimen of the breed falls short of the standard in some respect. It is virtually impossible for any dog to receive unanimous acclaim by everyone who compares it to the standard and to other dogs of the same breed. It is also impossible, even for a breeder or veterinarian, to tell how a puppy will shape up as an adult dog. The chances are that a puppy will inherit the qualities for which its father and mother (sire and dam) were bred, and if both parents and grandparents had good show records the puppy likely will have excellent possibilities.

Typically, a breed standard is drawn up by a national breed club (known as the parent club for that breed) and approved by the national kennel club, which is the governing body for purebred dogs in a particular country. Since any such standard is always subject to change, you should keep up with developments by checking publications of the appropriate club. You should also determine if

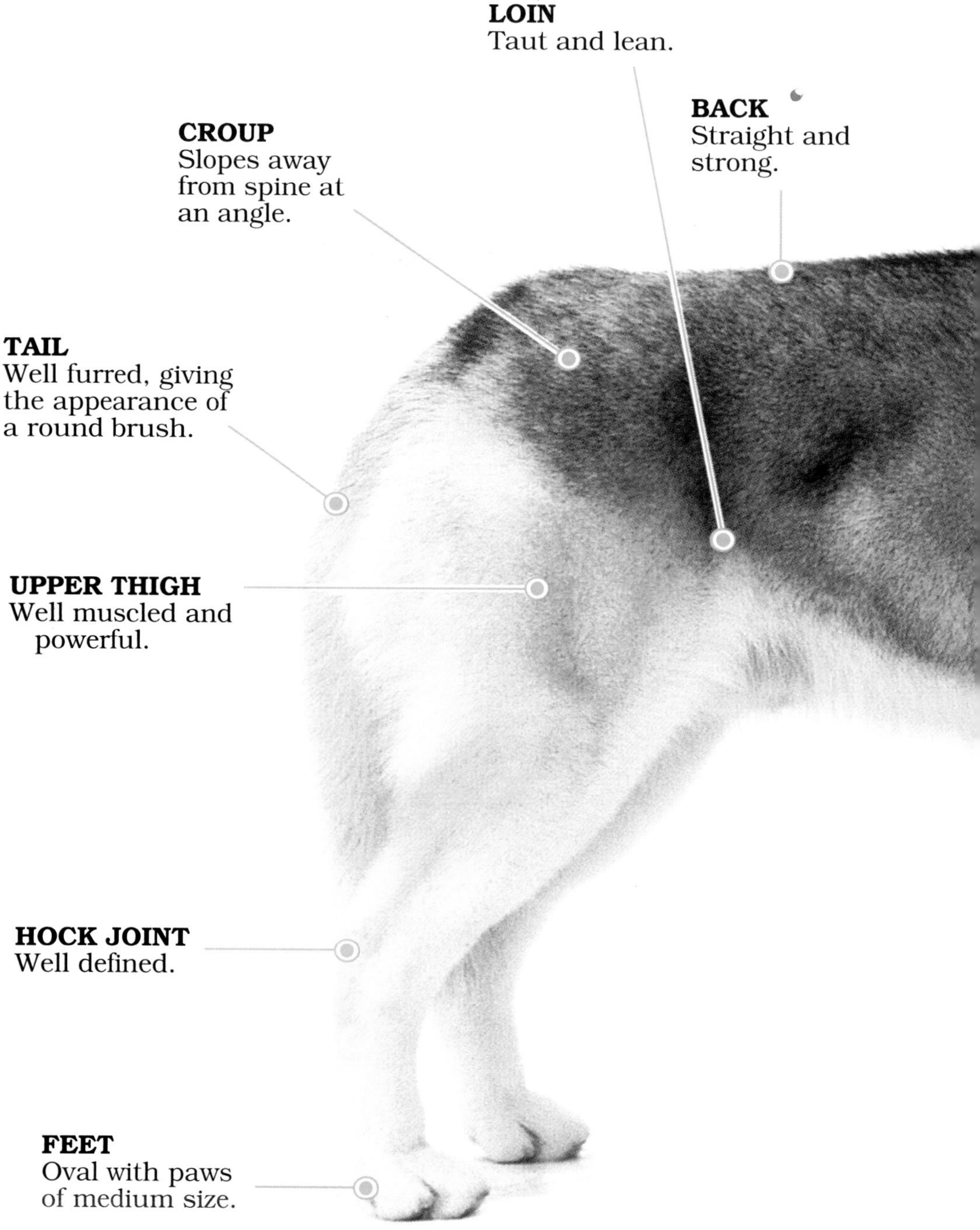

LOIN
Taut and lean.
BACK
Straight and strong.
CROUP
Slopes away from spine at an angle.
TAIL
Well furred, giving the appearance of a round brush.
UPPER THIGH
Well muscled and powerful.
HOCK JOINT
Well defined.
FEET
Oval with paws of medium size.

Ch. Kontoki's E-I-E-I-O, Westminster Kennel Club Best of Breed winner 1994 and 1995, owned by Nan Wisniewski, B. Moye, M. DePalma and T. Oelschlager.

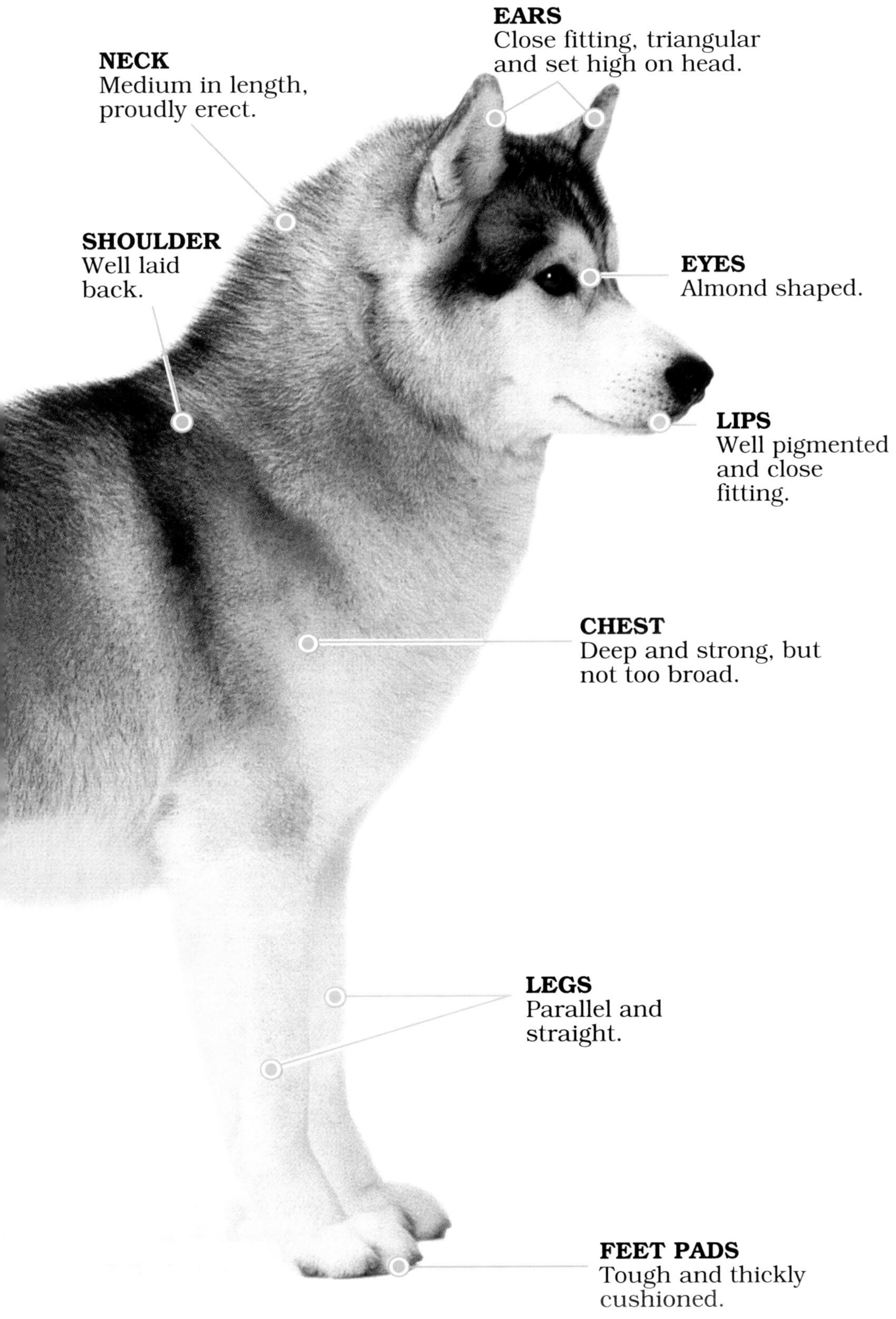

EARS
Close fitting, triangular
and set high on head.

NECK
Medium in length,
proudly erect.

SHOULDER
Well laid
back.

EYES
Almond shaped.

LIPS
Well pigmented
and close
fitting.

CHEST
Deep and strong, but
not too broad.

LEGS
Parallel and
straight.

FEET PADS
Tough and thickly
cushioned.

there is any particular information that may affect your decision to own a particular breed.

Following are the highlights of the American Kennel Club standard, provided here as a summary for easy reference.

SUMMARY OF THE AKC STANDARD

GENERAL APPEARANCE: The Siberian Husky is a medium-sized working dog, a northern breed, with moderately compact and well-furred body, erect ears and brush tail. He is quick and light on his feet and graceful and free in action: gait smooth and seemingly effortless. He can carry a light load at moderate speed over great distances.

His body proportion and form reflect this basic balance of

Darkly shaded color pattern on the skull, extending downward to the eyes. Also referred to as a "widow's peak." Drawing by John Quinn.

The Husky is a medium-sized working dog with a well-furred body, erect ears and brush tail.

The Siberian Husky must exhibit a straight strong back and a well-furred, fox-brush tail as the standard calls for.

straight, with elbows close to body and not turned in or out. Viewed from side, pasterns are slightly slanted, with pastern joint strong, but flexible. Bone is substantial but never heavy. Length of leg from elbow to ground is slightly more than distance from elbow to withers. Dewclaws on forelegs may be removed. (Faults: Weak pasterns; too heavy bone; too wide or too narrow in front; out at elbows.)

HIND LEGS: When standing and viewed from rear, hind legs are moderately spaced and parallel; upper thighs well-muscled and powerful, stifles well-bent, hock joint well-defined and set low to ground. Dewclaws, if any, are removed. (Faults: Straight stifles, cowhocks, too wide or too narrow in rear.)

FEET: Oval in shape, but not long. Paws are medium size,

Huskies are a natural breed and require few pre-show preparations. Bathing and brushing are all that is necessary.

Brush or Brushed tail is a tail covered in medium length bushy, stand-offish and brush-like coat, e.g., Siberian Husky. The hair on such a tail is of approximately the same length on the top, bottom and sides, giving the impression of a round bottom brush.

TAIL: Well-furred, fox-brush shape, set just below level of topline, usually carried over back in sickle curve when on attention. When carried up, tail does not curl to either side of body, or snap flat against back. A trailing tail is normal when working or in repose. Hair of medium length, approximately of same length on all sides, like a round brush. (Faults: Snapped or tightly curled tail; set too low or too high.)

compact and well-furred between toes and pads; pads tough and thickly cushioned; paws not turned in or out when on natural stance. (Faults: Soft or splayed toes; paws too large and clumsy; paws too small and delicate, toeing in or out.)

COAT: Double, of medium length, giving a well-furred appearance but not so long as to obscure dog's clear-cut outline. Undercoat is soft and dense and of sufficient length to support outer coat. Guard hairs of outer coat are straight, somewhat

The double coat of the Siberian Husky should give a well-furred appearance without obscuring the clear-cut outline of the body. Undercoat is soft and dense and of sufficient length to support the outer coat.

A variety of markings on the Siberian's head is common.

smooth-laying, never harsh or stand-off. Absence of undercoat during shedding time is normal. Trimming of whiskers and fur between toes and around feet permissible, but on any other part of body should be penalized. (Faults: Long, rough or shaggy coat; texture too harsh or too silky; trimming of coat, except as permitted.)

COLOR: All colors from black to white allowed. A variety of markings on head is common, including patterns not found in other breeds.

GAIT: Smooth and seemingly effortless. The Siberian Husky is quick and light on his feet, in the show ring he should be gaited on a loose leash at a moderately fast trot, showing good reach in forequarters and good drive in hindquarters. Seen from front to rear, at a walk he does not single track, but as speed increases the legs gradually angle inward until pads fall on a line directly under the longitudinal center of body. As pad marks converge, forelegs and hind legs are carried straight forward, with elbow and stifles not turned in or out. Each hind leg moves in the path of foreleg on each side. While gaiting, topline remains firm and level. (Faults: Short, prancing, or choppy gait; lumbering or rolling gait; crossing; crabbing.)

SIZE: Height: for dogs, 21 to 23 $^1/_2$ inches at withers; bitches, 20 to 22 inches. Weight: for dogs, 45 to 60 pounds; bitches, 35 to 50 pounds. Weight is in proportion to height. Measurements and weights are extreme limits, no preference given to them. (Disqualification: Dogs over 23 $^1/_2$ inches and bitches over 22 inches.)

Huskies are acceptable in all colors from black to white.

In addition to being friendly, gentle, alert, and outgoing, the Siberian Husky must also be able to get along with his fellow canines, as they will often work together as a team.

TEMPERAMENT: Friendly and gentle, also alert and outgoing. The Siberian Husky, unlike a guard dog, is not possessive, suspicious or aggressive. Reserve and dignity can be expected of a mature dog. His intelligence, tractability and eager disposition make him an agreeable companion and willing worker.

SUMMARY: Most important breed characteristics of the Siberian Husky: medium size, moderate bone, well-balanced proportions, ease and freedom of movement, proper coat, pleasing head and ears, correct tail and good disposition. The Siberian Husky is not so heavy or coarse like a freighting animal or so light and fragile like a sprint-racing animal. Both sexes appear capable of great endurance. In addition to faults cited, obvious structural faults common to all breeds are undesirable in the Siberian Husky, although not mentioned specifically.

YOUR NEW SIBERIAN HUSKY

SELECTION

When you do pick out a Siberian Husky puppy as a pet, don't be hasty; the longer you study puppies, the better you will understand them. Make it your transcendent concern to select only one that radiates good health and spirit and is lively on his feet, whose eyes are bright, whose coat shines, and who comes forward eagerly to make and to cultivate your acquaintance. Don't fall for any shy little darling that wants to retreat to his bed or his box, or plays coy behind other puppies or people, or hides his head under your arm or jacket appealing to your protective instinct. *Pick the Siberian Husky puppy who forthrightly picks you! The feeling of attraction should be mutual!*

DOCUMENTS

Now, a little paper work is in order. When you purchase a purebred Siberian Husky puppy, you should receive a transfer of ownership, registration material, and other "papers" (a list of the immunization shots, if any, the puppy may have been given; a note on whether or not the puppy has been wormed; a diet and feeding schedule to which

The young Siberian Husky is an aggressive chewer. Be sure to provide your puppy with a safe chew toy such as a Nylafloss®.

the puppy is accustomed) and you are welcomed as a fellow owner to a long, pleasant association with a most lovable pet, and more (news)paper work.

GENERAL PREPARATION

You have chosen to own a particular Siberian Husky puppy. You have chosen it very carefully over all other breeds and all other puppies. So before you ever get that Siberian Husky puppy home, you will have prepared for its arrival by reading everything you can get your hands on having to do with the management of Siberian Huskies and puppies. True, you will run into many conflicting opinions, but at least you will not be starting "blind." Read,

Play fighting is a fact of puppy life, and not something to be concerned about.

study, digest. Talk over your plans with your veterinarian, other "Siberian Husky people," and the seller of your Siberian Husky puppy.

When you get your Siberian Husky puppy, you will find that your reading and study are far from finished. You've just scratched the surface in your plan to provide the greatest possible comfort and health for your Siberian Husky; and, by the same token, you do want to assure yourself of the greatest possible enjoyment of this wonderful creature. You must be ready for this puppy mentally as well as in the physical requirements.

TRANSPORTATION

If you take the puppy home by car, protect him from drafts, particularly in cold weather. Wrapped in a towel and carried in the arms or lap of a passenger, the Siberian Husky puppy will usually make the trip without mishap. If the pup starts to drool and to squirm, stop the car for a few minutes. Have newspapers handy in case of car-sickness. A covered carton lined with newspapers provides protection for puppy and car, if you are driving alone. Avoid excitement and unnecessary handling of the puppy on arrival. A Siberian Husky puppy is a very small "package" to be making a complete change of surroundings and company, and

Though admittedly less picturesque, it is safer to transport your Siberian Husky in a properly sized crate rather than in a wicker basket.

Littermates spend every waking moment together - each puppy's first night in a new home is its first time alone.

THE FIRST DAY AND NIGHT

When your Siberian Husky puppy arrives in your home, put him down on the floor and don't pick him up again, except when it is absolutely necessary. He is a dog, a real dog, and must not be lugged around like a rag doll. Handle him as little as possible, and permit no one to pick him up and baby him. To repeat, *put your Siberian Husky puppy on the floor or the ground and let him stay there except when it may be necessary to do otherwise.*

Quite possibly your Siberian Husky puppy will be afraid for a while in his new surroundings, without his mother and littermates. Comfort him and reassure him, but don't console him. Don't give him the "oh-you-poor-itsy-bitsy-puppy" treatment. Be calm, friendly, and reassuring. Encourage him to walk around

he needs frequent rest and refreshment to renew his vitality.

A wading pool is the perfect size and shape for whelping puppies.

Keep track of your puppy's weight gain. He should not lose weight as he grows but he should not become obese either.

there in good proportions; and be especially certain that the food contains properly high levels of vitamins A and D, two of the most perishable and important ones. Note the B-complex level, but don't worry about carbohydrate and mineral levels. These substances are plentiful and cheap and not likely to be lacking in a good brand.

The advice given for how to choose a dry food also applies to moist or canned types of dog foods, if you decide to feed one of these.

Having chosen a really good food, feed it to your Siberian Husky as the manufacturer directs. And once you've started, stick to it. Never change if you can possibly help it. A switch from one meal or kibble-type food can usually be made without too much upset; however, a change will almost invariably give you (and your Siberian Husky) some trouble.

Your Husky's coat quality and overall health are a relfection of the food you choose to offer him.

WHEN SUPPLEMENTS ARE NEEDED

Now what about supplements of various kinds, mineral and vitamin, or the various oils? They are all okay to add to your Siberian Husky's food. However, if you are feeding your Siberian Husky a correct diet, and this is easy to do, no supplements are necessary unless your Siberian Husky has been improperly fed, Husky! The same risk goes with minerals.

FEEDING SCHEDULE

When and how much food to give your Siberian Husky? As to when (except in the instance of puppies), suit yourself. You may feed two meals per day or the same amount in one single feeding, either morning or night.

Newborn Huskies acquire all the nourishment from their dam. The weaning process begins at approximately four week.

has been sick, or is having puppies. Vitamins and minerals are naturally present in all the foods; and to ensure against any loss through processing, they are added in concentrated form to the dog food you use. Except on the advice of your veterinarian, added amounts of vitamins can prove harmful to your Siberian

As to how to prepare the food and how much to give, it is generally best to follow the directions on the food package. Your own Siberian Husky may want a little more or a little less.

Fresh, cool water should always be available to your Siberian Husky. This is important to good health throughout his lifetime.

Fresh, cool water is an absolute necessity when your Siberian Husky is outdoors on a hot sunny day.

The Nylabone/Gumabone® Pooch Pacifiers enable the dog to slowly chew off the knobs while they clean their own teeth. The knobs develop elastic frays which act as a toothbrush. These pacifiers are extremely effective as detailed scientific studies have shown.

ALL SIBERIAN HUSKIES NEED TO CHEW

Puppies and young Siberian Huskys need something with resistance to chew on while their teeth and jaws are developing— for cutting the puppy teeth, to induce growth of the permanent teeth under the puppy teeth, to assist in getting rid of the puppy teeth at the proper time, to help the permanent teeth through the gums, to ensure normal jaw development, and to settle the permanent teeth solidly in the jaws.

The adult Siberian Husky's desire to chew stems from the instinct for tooth cleaning, gum massage, and jaw exercise—plus the need for an outlet for periodic doggie tensions.

This is why dogs, especially puppies and young dogs, will often destroy property worth hundreds of dollars when their chewing instinct is not diverted from their owner's possessions. And this is why you should provide your Siberian Husky with something to chew—something that has the necessary functional qualities, is desirable from the Siberian Husky's viewpoint, and is safe for him.

It is very important that your Siberian Husky not be permitted to chew on anything he can break or on any indigestible thing from which he can bite sizable chunks. Sharp pieces, such as from a bone which can be broken by a dog, may pierce the intestinal wall and kill. Indigestible things that can be bitten off in chunks, such as from shoes or rubber or plastic toys, may cause an intestinal

Young puppies need their instincts directed in constructive ways.

stoppage (if not regurgitated) and bring painful death, unless surgery is promptly performed.

Pet shops sell real bones which have been colored, cooked, dyed or served natural. Some of the bones are huge, but they usually are easily destroyed and become very dangerous.

Strong natural bones, such as 4- to 8-inch lengths of round shin bone from mature beef—either the kind you can get from a butcher or one of the variety available commercially in pet stores— may serve your Siberian Husky's teething needs if his mouth is large enough to handle them effectively. You may be tempted to give your puppy a smaller bone and he may not be able to break it when you do, but puppies grow rapidly and the power of their jaws constantly increases until maturity. This means that a growing Husky may break one

A chicken-flavored Gumabone has tiny particles of chicken powder embedded in it to keep the Siberian Husky interested.

of the smaller bones at any time, swallow the pieces, and die painfully before you realize what is wrong.

All hard natural bones are very abrasive. If your Siberian Husky is an avid chewer, natural bones may wear away his teeth prematurely; hence, they then should be taken away from your dog when the teething purposes have been served. The badly worn, and usually painful, teeth of many dogs can be traced to excessive chewing on natural bones.

Contrary to popular belief, knuckle bones that can be chewed up and swallowed by your Siberian Husky provide little, if any, usable calcium or other

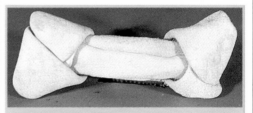

Rawhide is probably the best-selling dog chew. It can be dangerous and cause a dog to choke on it as it swells when wet. A molded, melted rawhide mixed with casein is available (though always scarce).

nutriment. They do, however, disturb the digestion of most dogs and cause them to vomit the nourishing food they need.

Dried rawhide products of various types, shapes, sizes, and prices are available on the market and have become quite popular. However, they don't serve the primary chewing functions very well; they are a bit messy when wet from mouthing, and most Siberian Huskies chew them up rather rapidly—but they have been considered safe for dogs until recently. Now, more and more incidents of death, and near death, by strangulation have been reported to be the results of partially swallowed chunks of rawhide swelling in the throat. More recently, some veterinarians have been attributing cases of acute constipation to large pieces of incompletely digested rawhide in the intestine.

A new product, molded rawhide, is very safe. During the process, the rawhide is melted and then injection molded into the familiar dog shape. It is very hard and is eagerly accepted by Siberian Huskies. The melting process also sterilizes the rawhide. Don't confuse this with pressed rawhide, which is nothing more than small strips of rawhide squeezed together.

The nylon bones, especially those with natural meat and bone fractions added, are probably the most complete, safe, and economical answer to the chewing need. Dogs cannot break them or bite off sizable chunks; hence, they are completely safe—and being longer lasting than other things offered for the purpose,

Keeping your Siberian Husky healthy and happy takes a lot more than feeding a proper diet. Be sure to exercise your Husky outdoors on a regular basis to maintain vibrance.

they are economical.

Hard chewing raises little bristle-like projections on the surface of the nylon bones—to provide effective interim tooth cleaning and vigorous gum massage, much in the same way your toothbrush does it for you. The little projections are raked off and swallowed in the form of thin shavings, but the chemistry of the nylon is such that they break down in the stomach fluids and pass through without effect.

The toughness of the nylon provides the strong chewing resistance needed for important jaw exercise and effectively aids teething functions, but there is no tooth wear because nylon is non-abrasive. Being inert, nylon does not support the growth of

Chocolate Nylabone® has a one micron thickness coat of chocolate under the skin of the nylon. When the Siberian Husky chews it the white subsurface is exposed. This photo shows before and after chewing.

Most pet shops have complete walls dedicated to safe pacifiers.

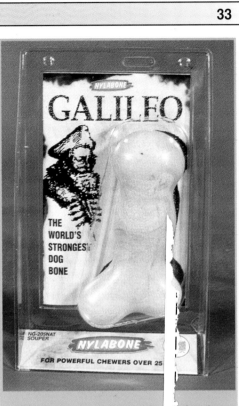

The Galileo is an extremely tough nylon pacifier. Its design is based upon original sketches by Galileo. A book explaining the history and workings of the design come inside each package. This might very well be the best design for a Siberian Husky.

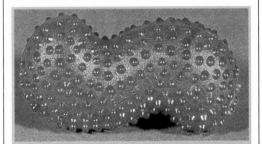

Siberian Huskies have such strong jaws that most ordinary pacifiers (chew devices) are immediately destroyed. The Hercules has been designed with Siberian Huskies and other large breeds in mind. This bone is made of polyurethane, like car bumpers.

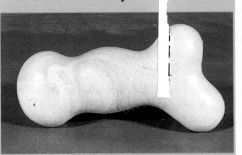

Raised dental tips on each dog bone works wonders with controlling plaque in a Siberian Husky.

Only get the largest plaque attacker for your Siberian Husky.

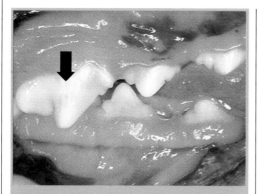

In a scientific study, this shows a dog's tooth while being maintained by Gumabone chewing.

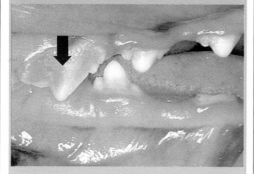

The Gumabone was taken away and in 30 days the tooth was almost completely covered with plaque and tartar.

microorganisms; and it can be washed in soap and water or it can be sterilized by boiling or in an autoclave.

Nylabone® is highly recommended by veterinarians as a safe, healthy nylon bone that can't splinter or chip. Nylabone® is frizzled by the dog's chewing action, creating a toothbrush-like surface that cleanses the teeth and massages the gums. Nylabone®, the only chew products made of flavor-impregnated solid nylon, are available in your local pet shop. Nylabone® is superior to the cheaper bones because it is made

of virgin nylon, which is the strongest and longest-lasting type of nylon available. The cheaper bones are made from recycled or re-ground nylon scraps, and have a tendency to break apart and split easily.

Nothing, however, substitutes for periodic professional attention for your Siberian Husky's teeth and gums, not any more than your toothbrush can do that for you. Have your Siberian Husky's teeth cleaned at least once a year by your veterinarian (twice a year is better) and he will be happier, healthier, and far more pleasant to live with.

The nylon tug toy is actually a dental floss. You grab one end and let your Siberian Husky tug on the other as it slowly slips through his teeth since nylon is self-lubricating (slippery). Do NOT use cotton rope tug toys as cotton is organic and rots. It is also weak and easily loses strands which are indigestible should the dog swallow them.

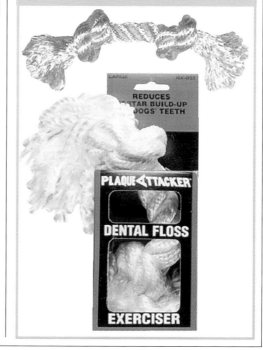

TRAINING YOUR SIBERIAN

You owe proper training to your Siberian Husky. The right and privilege of being trained is his birthright; and whether your Siberian Husky is going to be a handsome, well-mannered housedog and companion, a show dog, or whatever possible use he may be put to, the basic training is always the same—all must start with basic obedience, or what might be called "manner training."

Your Siberian Husky must come instantly when called and obey the

PROFESSIONAL TRAINING

How do you go about this training? Well, it's a very simple procedure, pretty well standardized by now. First, if you can afford the extra expense, you may send your Siberian Husky to a professional trainer, where in 30 to 60 days he will learn how to be a "good dog." If you enlist the services of a good professional trainer, follow his advice of when to come to see the dog. No, he

Only use Frisbees with a dog bone molded on the top. This shows the Frisbee was made for dogs and is safe for them to chew on (which they always do!). The Nylabone® also helps the dog get a grip on the Frisbee if it lands flat on a smooth surface.
* The trademark Frisbee is used under license from Matell, Inc., California, USA.

"Sit" or "Down" command just as fast; he must walk quietly at "Heel," whether on or off lead. He must be mannerly and polite wherever he goes; he must be polite to strangers on the street and in stores. He must be mannerly in the presence of other dogs. He must not bark at children, motorcycles, or other domestic animals. And he must be restrained from chasing cats. It is not a dog's inalienable right to chase cats, and he must be reprimanded for it.

won't forget you, but too-frequent visits at the wrong time may slow down his training progress. And using a "pro" trainer means that you will have to go for some training, too, after the trainer feels your Siberian Husky is ready to go home. You will have to learn how your Siberian Husky works, just what to expect of him and how to use what the dog has learned after he is home.

OBEDIENCE TRAINING CLASS

Another way to train your Siberian Husky (many experienced Siberian Husky people think this is the best) is to join an obedience training class right in your own community. There is such a group in nearly every community nowadays. Here you will be working with a group of people who are also just starting out. You will actually be training your own dog, since all work is done under the direction of a head trainer who will make suggestions to you and also tell you when and how to correct your Siberian Husky's errors. Then, too, working with such a group, your Siberian Husky will learn to get along with other dogs. And, what is more important, he will learn to do exactly what he is told to do, no matter how much

Leash training and heeling are fundamental to enjoying outdoor time with your Siberian Husky.

confusion there is around him or how great the temptation is to go his own way.

Write to your national kennel club for the location of a training club or class in your locality. Sign up. Go to it regularly—every session! Go early and leave late! Both you and your Siberian Husky will benefit tremendously.

TRAIN HIM BY THE BOOK

The third way of training your Siberian Husky is by the book. Yes, you can do it this way and do a good job of it too. If you can read and if you're smarter than the dog, you'll do a good job. But in using the book method, select a book, buy it, study it carefully; then study it some more, until the procedures are almost second nature to you. Then start your training. But stay with the book and its advice and exercises. Don't start in and then make up a few rules of your own. If you don't

Obedience training with your Siberian puppy begins with basic commands and is always filled with praise.

The athletic Siberian Husky can learn to perform agility tasks such as the bar jump.

follow the book, you'll get into jams you can't get out of by yourself. If after a few hours of short training sessions your Siberian Husky is still not working as he should, get back to the book for a study session, because it's your fault, not the dog's! The procedures of dog training have been so well systemized that it must be your fault, since literally thousands of fine Siberian Huskies have been trained by the book.

After your Siberian Husky is "letter perfect" under all conditions, then, if you wish, go on to advanced training and trick work.

Your Siberian Husky will love his obedience training, and you'll burst with pride at the finished product! Your Siberian Husky will enjoy life even more, and you'll enjoy your Siberian Husky more. And remember— you *owe good training to your Siberian Husky.*

While training and physical ability affects a dog's sledding potential, geneology is the key factor.

TRAINING YOUR SLED DOG

Just as the Bloodhound has an inherent desire and ability to sniff out game, the Siberian Husky has the instinctual pleasure and talent to pull a sled across cavernous terrain of ice and snow. Because of his stamina and sustained power over long

Husky puppy will one day be leading a pack of dogs on the Iditarod—not by a long shot. First of all, the genetics of your dog has a lot to do with his ability to race competitively. Chances are, if your dog's parents were champion sled dogs, your new little Husky

This young Husky's parents were excellent sled dogs—chances are he'll be pulling with champions in no time.

distances, the Siberian Husky is probably the best breed for pulling, carting, and racing. The racing of sled dogs is still a popular and competitive sport, and the Siberian Husky has remained the foremost breed of choice.

However, geneology alone does not mean that your Siberian

may have what it takes to be a top puller himself someday. If not, that doesn't mean that he can't have a grand old time pulling in areas other than Alaska. After all, pulling is the task he was selectively bred to do, and he will enjoy it anywhere. Whether you're interested in competing with a real sled-dog team or you just want to have fun letting your Siberian Husky pull a wagon around the yard, you still must teach your dog a few simple commands and condition him through a basic training program.

PREREQUISITES

Not that much is required to begin your Husky in basic sled training. For the most part, your dog should be of typical racing type; that is, sound, well balanced, and well angulated. Well angulated for racing and pulling means that the dog has longer legs and lighter bones than some heavier dogs you might see in conformation showing. Generally speaking, a good racing Husky weighs under 60 pounds with good feet and a lean build. However, if you're just pulling for fun, all that is required of your Husky is that he be sound, healthy, and have an innate desire to run.

The first purchase you'll need to make is a well-fitting harness. Don't skimp on this! Cheaper, one-size-fits-all harnesses just won't cut it. One size does not fit

A good racing dog weighs 60 pounds— without the hat!

all, because all dogs have different sized necks. Pulling a sled is enjoyable for your Husky but also a very difficult task—there is no reason to make it any harder for him. The least you can do is put enough effort into buying a harness that fits him properly. To get an idea of how the harness is supposed to fit, attend a dog sled race, weight pull or carting competition. Talk to some of the people about what they look for in a harness. Look at the dogs in harness and take note of where the stress points are. Also notice what type of material the harness is made of. The more expensive harnesses are made of leather, but there are affordable ones made of nylon and other materials. For the beginning puller, you will want to start with something that is soft and comfortable. If your dog is uncomfortable in his harness, he will quickly lose interest in pulling anything. The best option is to purchase a custom-fit harness from a reputable producer/ supplier. Respectable pet

Even if the younger dogs in the pack are not going to pull, bring them along for the experience—dogs learn by watching!

equipment companies can be found advertised in the back of almost any large dog magazine.

The only other things you need besides a harness is a willing dog and something to pull. Any draggable object will do in the beginning, such as a small log or an old tire. Eventually you will want your Husky to pull a rolling object, in which case a cart or a wagon are both excellent options.

Start with a soft harness and let him drag a small log or wooden board around. Judge the weight of the log/board in relation to the weight of the dog. If your puppy really struggles to pull, then the weight is too heavy. Too vigorous a struggle will cause your puppy to lose interest. On the other hand, don't give him a log that's so light it will catch up with him when he's pulling downhill. He

Pulling is hard work—allow a beginner dog time to rest between practice runs.

EARLY TRAINING

Once you have found a good harness, you are ready to begin training. Regardless of whether your Siberian Husky will race, pull weight, or both, training can begin around two or three months of age. Beginning any earlier could be detrimental to the bones and joints of your growing puppy.

must understand that there is some kind of effort in pulling, and that he's not just running around with something following him. So, try to find a happy medium between the two extremes, and monitor your puppy's behavior as he's pulling. Of course, as your puppy continues to grow and gets more accustomed to pulling weights, you can make necessary adjustments to the load.

During the time your Siberian Husky puppy is learning to pull, encourage him to pull along a set path. He should be taught to follow a trail or a straight line; otherwise he will run around aimlessly and without cause. Developing his pulling skills with a planned route in mind will make transition to racing or pulling competition effortless should you of training will be finding a place to train your Siberian Husky. Of course, a local dog track is the ideal place to be, but not everyone lives near such a place. Try to find a park, wooded area, or open field where dogs can run a distance with minimum danger and smooth terrain. Check out the area you choose before training your dog, with an eye out for hazardous objects such as glass, debris, ditches, jagged

Sledding afficionados will likely have to drive many miles from home to find a suitable locale for their Huskies to do their thing.

ever decide to go that route in the future. Remember, teaching any type of skill is most effective during puppyhood, so teach him the right way from the beginning.

THE NEED FOR SPACE

Unless you are fortunate enough to live on five acres of farmland, the most difficult aspect rocks, thorny brush, sudden drops, and the like. By no means should you ever train your dog in a parking lot! Hard concrete surfaces irritate the pads of a dog's feet, which in turn causes the dog to run with a hackneyed gait to save his feet. Obviously, this type of adjustment prevents the dog from reaching his full

Select an area that is free of distractions for your team to run.

stride and could possibly cause muscle and/or joint injuries. Ideally, you'd want to train your Husky on snow or sand, but if those conditions are not available, then a dirt surface is acceptable.

Also try to avoid any areas where there is a large population of wild animals. Besides the danger of getting bitten, you don't want your Husky deciding he'd rather chase a pack of rabbits than perform the task at hand. Which brings up one of the most important factors to consider when choosing a practice area: distractions. Try to find an area that will not be filled with people, children, other pets, etc., for two reasons. First of all, there is the matter of safety—people rightly

will feel fear if a 60-pound dog comes tearing at them at full speed. Secondly, you must get your dog's undivided attention. Populated areas provide distractions that are too inviting for your dog to ignore, especially if he is a puppy or young dog. A puppy's short attention span is difficult enough to work with, so if the area you find is not always empty, figure out a time that it is, such as early morning.

TRAINING RULES

One issue important to the understanding of any kind of training is this: do not teach too many commands. As eager to learn as puppies are, keep in mind that they cannot retain too many words, and expecting too much of them too soon will only confuse them and likely cause them to lose interest. Always praise them profusely with petting and a high tone of voice when

Siberian Huskies take a well-deserved break during practice.

they accomplish the assigned task—this type of positive reinforcement has a much stronger effect than negativity ever could. Stick to very basic rules that apply to training of any kind. For example, do not feed or water immediately before training, and be sure to allow your Husky sessions. Even if you're not going to become a professional dog racer, you still should work with your dog on a regular basis; if not once a day, then every other day at the least. This does not mean you must follow a strict regimen of three-hour training sessions. Quite the contrary; you will get

A Husky sled team reined up and ready to run.

to exercise a while before you get into the actual commands and work. Also, and maybe most importantly, do not attempt to teach another command or lesson until the dog has already learned the last one.

Once you have begun a training program, remember it is exactly that: a program. This means that there is consistency and discipline in the scheduling of your much better results from your dog through very short sessions on a regular basis than with a few extensive workouts spread out over a week. Training should be a joy for both the Husky and the owner and should not be considered a chore. Keeping to a daily routine not only will produce a healthy, happy Husky but also will develop a strong bond between you and your loyal companion.

At two years of age, this Husky glistens with experience at the peak of his training.

Depending on how serious you want to train, you should be aware of your dog's limits. Your Husky, like most dogs, will probably work as long as you ask him to, which means you have to decide when he's too tired to continue. A healthy Siberian Husky puppy is capable of covering about a mile of terrain without too much strain by the time he is eight months old. Because Huskies will usually pace themselves when running over long distances, it is a good idea to steadily increase the training distance each day. This strategy will increase your dog's desire to "go further" and reach the finish line. Should you stick to a serious training regimen, the Husky is able to cover 15 to 16 miles at the peak of his training and performance at the age of two years.

PROFESSIONAL RACING

As you might imagine, racing in regional meets for fun is entirely different from professional sled-dog racing, where there are high stakes to win. For those involved with sled-dog teams, racing is their profession, their livelihood. The lives of their dogs are dedicated to winning and little else. Therefore, the training is rigorous, culling ruthless, and

Professional racing is exorbitantly expensive and extremely time-consuming. However, there are a number of fun competitions that you can enter through your local Husky club.

expenses exorbitant. Even though the purses won at big dog races are very high, the costs of maintaining a professional team far exceed the winnings. Team owners spare no expense to feed top-grade beef to their dogs or to travel across the world to participate in an event. A top-notch trained sled dog can cost the price of a new car, depending on its ability and past performances.

While there are more Siberian Huskies on professional racing teams now than ever before, there are not as many as you might expect. There are at least two reasons for this fact. First of all, pro teams are interested in any dog, purebred or otherwise, that can run fast enough to bring them the prize money. So, there is no loyalty to one breed; all that matters is that the dog competes and runs well with the other dogs on the team. Secondly, purebred Siberian Huskies are very costly to breed and maintain; for some team owners it is not economically efficient to use Huskies exclusively if a lower-

priced yet suitable halfbreed can be found.

Chances are, you are not interested in forming a professional sled-dog team. However, that doesn't mean you and your Siberian Husky can't enjoy the thrill of competition and the satisfaction of winning. Local clubs often sponsor various events, including racing, carting, and other fun activities, that both you and your Siberian Husky can enjoy. Write to your local breed club for information on how you can get involved.

Other draft dogs, such as the Alaskan Malamute and crossbreeds, have replaced the Siberian Husky on many professional racing teams.

SHOWING YOUR SIBERIAN

A show Siberian Husky is a comparatively rare thing. He is one out of several litters of puppies. He happens to be born with a degree of physical perfection that closely approximates the standard by which the breed is judged in the show ring. Such a dog should, on maturity, be able to win or approach his champion- ship in good, fast company at the larger shows. Upon finishing his championship, he is apt to be as highly desirable as a breeding animal. As a proven stud, he will automatically command a high price for service.

Showing Siberian Huskies is a lot of fun—yes, but it is a highly competitive sport. While all the experts were once

Gaiting the Husky in the show ring is the true test of sound structure.

beginners, the odds are against a novice. You will be showing against experienced handlers, often people who have devoted a lifetime to breeding, picking the right ones, and then showing those dogs through to their championships. Moreover, the most perfect Siberian Husky ever born has faults, and in your hands the faults will be far more evident than with the experienced handler who knows how to minimize his Siberian Husky's faults. These are but a few points on the sad side of the picture.

The experienced handler, as I say, was not born knowing the ropes. He learned—*and so can you!* You can if you will put in the same time, study and keen observation that he did. But it will take time!

KEY TO SUCCESS

First, search for a truly fine show prospect. Take the puppy home, raise him by the book, and as carefully as you know how, give him every chance to mature into the Siberian Husky you hoped for. My advice is to keep your dog out of big shows, even Puppy Classes, until he is mature. Maturity in the male is roughly two years; with the female, 14 months or so. When your Siberian Husky is approaching maturity, start out at match shows, and, with this experience for both of you, then go gunning for the big wins at the big shows.

Next step, read the standard by which the Siberian Husky is judged. Study it until you know it by heart. Having done this, and while your puppy is at home (where he should be) growing into a normal, healthy Siberian Husky, go to every dog show you can possibly reach. Sit at the ringside and watch Siberian Husky judging. Keep your ears and eyes open. Do your own judging, holding each of those dogs against the standard, which you now know by heart.

In your evaluations, don't start looking for faults. Look for the virtues—the best qualities. How does a given Siberian Husky shape up against the standard? Having looked for and noted the virtues, then note the faults and see what prevents a given Siberian Husky from standing correctly or moving well. Weigh these faults against the virtues, since, ideally, every feature of the dog should contribute to the harmonious whole dog.

"RINGSIDE JUDGING"

It's a good practice to make notes on each Siberian Husky, always holding the dog against the standard. In "ringside judging," forget your personal preference for this or that feature. What does the standard say about it? Watch carefully as the judge places the dogs in a given class. It is difficult from the ringside

The decision to show a Siberian Husky should be made before you have selected a puppy. If you do intend to exhibit, it will be necessary to pick a top-quality pup.

always to see why number one was placed over the second dog. Try to follow the judge's reasoning. Later try to talk with the judge after he is finished. Ask him questions as to why he placed certain Siberian Huskies and not others. Listen while the judge explains his placings, and, I'll say right here, any judge

personal progress if you are a good listener.

THE NATIONAL CLUB

You will find it worthwhile to join the National Siberian Husky club and to subscribe to its magazine. From the national club, you will learn the location of an approved regional club near you.

Siberian Huskies and their handlers competing in the ring. Before you begin showing, you should attend as many shows as you possibly can and take notes on the procedures and etiquette.

worthy of his license should be able to give reasons.

When you're not at the ringside, talk with the fanciers and breeders who have Siberian Huskies. Don't be afraid to ask opinions or say that you don't know. You have a lot of listening to do, and it will help you a great deal and speed up your

Now, when your young Siberian Husky is eight to ten months old, find out the dates of match shows in your section of the country. These differ from regular shows only in that no championship points are given. These shows are especially designed to launch new dogs (and young handlers) on a show career.

ENTER MATCH SHOWS

With the ring deportment you have watched at big shows firmly in mind and practice, enter your Siberian Husky in as many match shows as you can. When in the ring, you have two jobs. One is to see to it that your Siberian Husky is always being seen to its best advantage. The other job is to keep your eye on answer his questions. If he does something you don't like, don't say so. And don't irritate the judge (and everybody else) by constantly talking and fussing with your dog.

In moving about the ring, remember to keep clear of dogs beside you or in front of you. It is my advice to you *not* to show your Siberian Husky in a regular

The ideal Siberian Husky show prospect conforms very closely to the standard. This Husky exhibits excellent conformation.

the judge to see what he may want you to do next. Watch only the judge and your Siberian Husky. Be quick and be alert; do exactly as the judge directs. Don't speak to him except to point show until he is at least close to maturity and after both you and your dog have had time to perfect ring manners and poise in the match shows.

YOUR HEALTHY HUSKY

We know our pets, their moods and habits, and therefore we can recognize when our Siberian Husky is experiencing an off-day. Signs of sickness can be very obvious or very subtle. As any mother can attest, diagnosing and treating an ailment require common sense, knowing when to seek home remedies and when to visit your doctor....or veterinarian, as the case may be.

Your veterinarian, we know, is your Siberian Husky's best friend, next to you. It will pay to be choosy about your veterinarian. Talk to dog-owning friends whom you respect. Visit more than one vet before you make a lifelong choice. Trust your instincts. Find a knowledgeable, compassionate vet who knows Siberian Huskies and likes them.

Grooming for good health makes good sense. The Siberian Husky's coat is double and medium in length. The dense outer coat benefits from regular brushing to keep looking glossy and clean. Brushing stimulates the natural oils in the coat and also removes dead haircoat. Siberian Huskies shed seasonally, which means their undercoat (the soft downy white fur) is pushed out by the incoming new coat. A medium-strength bristle brush is all that is required to groom this

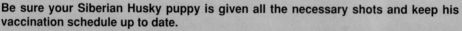

Be sure your Siberian Husky puppy is given all the necessary shots and keep his vaccination schedule up to date.

beautiful breed of dog. Frequent brushing can help minimize many of the skin-related problems which can plague the Husky. Among this disorders are zinc-deficiency disorders, dermatitis, patchy coat and hot spots. Hot spots or eczema occur during the summer months, frequently near the hindquarters where the curled tail rests on the ham. They are easily treated, though not pleasant.

Anal sacs, sometimes called anal glands, are located in the musculature of the anal ring, one on either side. Each empties into the rectum via a small duct. Occasionally their secretion becomes thickened and accumulates so you can readily feel these structures from the outside. If your Siberian Husky is scooting across the floor dragging his rear quarters, or licking his rear, his anal sacs may need to be expressed. Placing pressure in and up towards the anus, while holding the tail, is the general routine. Anal sac secretions are characteristically foul-smelling, and you could get squirted if not careful. Veterinarians can take care of this during regular visits and demonstrate the cleanest method.

The summer months can be cruel to your Siberian Husky. Make sure your Husky gets plenty of water and an occasional hose-down when he is in the heat for extensive periods, such as during an outdoor dog show.

Summer months are the cruelest months for Huskies, as their natural tolerance to heat is less than that of most breeds. It is true that their coats provide insulation as well as cooling, yet the dogs simply were not bred to endure tropical temperatures. Plenty of water to drink and regular hosing down can help make your Huskies summer a healthy and tolerable one. Never leave a Husky (or any dog) directly in the sunlight without refuge of shade. Heatstroke affects many dogs and is a frequent killer in the good old summertime.

Although hip dysplasia (HD) is a common problem in most purebred dogs, fortunately the Siberian Husky suffers from a fairly low occurrence rate. Breeders have been careful about screening certificates from such hip registries as OFA or PennHIP. Since HD is hereditary, it's necessary to know that the parents and grandparents of your puppy had hips rated good or better. Dysplastic dogs suffer from badly constructed hip joints which become arthritic and very painful, thereby hindering the dog's ability to be a working dog, a good-moving show dog, or even a happy, active pet.

The primary concern of Husky breeders is eye conditions, such as corneal dystrophy, cataracts, and progressive retinal atrophy (PRA). Screening for eye problems has therefore been prioritized.

Overall, a well-bred Siberian Husky is a healthy, long-lived companion animal. Proper care and education can only help owners promote the health and longevity of their dogs. Most breeders advise against feeding the Siberian Husky one large meal per day because of the dangers of bloat (gastric torsion), the twisting of the stomach causes gas to build up and the organ expands like a balloon. Avoiding strenuous exercise and large amounts of water can preclude the occurrence of bloat, as can feeding

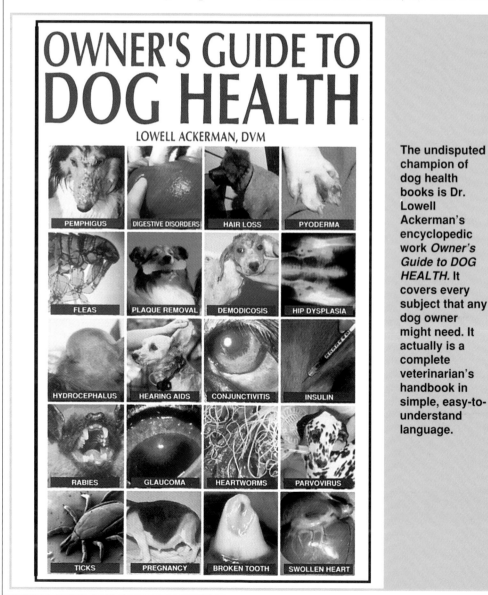

OWNER'S GUIDE TO
DOG HEALTH
LOWELL ACKERMAN, DVM

PEMPHIGUS | DIGESTIVE DISORDERS | HAIR LOSS | PYODERMA
FLEAS | PLAQUE REMOVAL | DEMODICOSIS | HIP DYSPLASIA
HYDROCEPHALUS | HEARING AIDS | CONJUNCTIVITIS | INSULIN
RABIES | GLAUCOMA | HEARTWORMS | PARVOVIRUS
TICKS | PREGNANCY | BROKEN TOOTH | SWOLLEN HEART

The undisputed champion of dog health books is Dr. Lowell Ackerman's encyclopedic work *Owner's Guide to DOG HEALTH.* It covers every subject that any dog owner might need. It actually is a complete veterinarian's handbook in simple, easy-to-understand language.

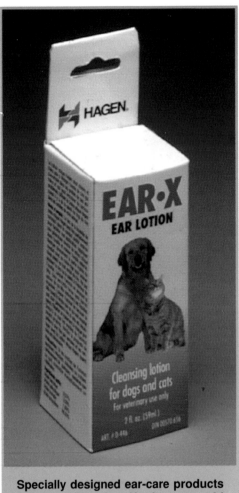

Specially designed ear-care products for your Siberian Husky are sold through most pet shops. Photograph courtesy of Hagen.

hepatitis, leptospirosis, adenovirus, parainfluenza, coronavirus, bordetella, tracheobronchitis (kennel cough), Lyme disease and rabies.

Parvovirus is a highly contagious, dog-specific disease, first recognized in 1978. Targeting the small intestine, parvo affects the stomach, and diarrhea and vomiting (with blood) are clinical signs. Although the dog can pass the infection to other dogs within three days of infection, the initial signs, which include lethargy and depression, don't display themselves until four to seven days. When affecting puppies under four weeks of age, the heart muscle is frequently attacked. When the heart is affected, the puppies exhibit difficulty in breathing and experience crying and foaming at the nose and mouth.

Distemper, related to human measles, is an airborne virus that spreads in the blood and ultimately in the nervous system and epithelial tissues. Young dogs or dogs with weak immune systems can develop encephalomyelitis (brain disease) from the distemper infection. Such dogs experience seizures, general weakness and rigidity, as well as "hardpad." Since distemper is largely incurable, prevention through vaccination is vitally important. Puppies should be vaccinated at six to eight weeks of age, with boosters at ten to 12 weeks. Older puppies (16 weeks and older) who are unvaccinated should receive no fewer than two vaccinations at three- to four-week intervals.

two smaller meals instead of one larger one. A good commercial dog food is recommended for the dog's balanced diet.

For the continued health of your dog, owners must attend to vaccinations regularly. Your veterinarian can recommend a vaccination schedule appropriate for your dog, taking into consideration the factors of climate and geography. The basic vaccinations to protect your dog are: parvovirus, distemper,

Hepatitis mainly affects the liver and is caused by canine adenovirus type I. Highly infectious, hepatitis often affects dogs nine to 12 months of age. Initially the virus localizes in the dog's tonsils and then disperses to the liver, kidney and eyes. Generally speaking the dog's immune system is capable of combating this virus. Canine infectious hepatitis affects dogs whose systems cannot fight off the adenovirus. Affected dogs have fever, abdominal pains, bruising on mucous membranes and gums, and experience coma and convulsions. Prevention of hepatitis exists only through vaccination at eight to ten weeks of age and then boosters three or four weeks later, then annually.

Leptospirosis is a bacterium-related disease, often spread by rodents. The organisms that spread leptospirosis enter through the mucous membranes and spread to the internal organs via the bloodstream. It can be passed through the dog's urine. Leptospirosis does not affect young dogs as consistently as do the other viruses; it is reportedly regional in distribution and somewhat dependent on the immunostatus of the dog. Fever, inappetence, vomiting, dehydration, hemorrhage, kidney and eye disease can result in moderate cases.

Bordetella, called canine cough, causes a persistent hacking

Carefully inspect your Husky's coat for parasites after he has been outdoors for a lengthy period of time.

cough in dogs and is very contagious. Bordetella involves a virus and a bacteria: parainfluenza is the most common virus implicated; *Bordetella bronchiseptica*, the bacterium. Bronchitis and pneumonia result in less than 20 percent of the cases, and most dogs recover from the condition within a week to four weeks. Non-prescription medicines can help relieve the hacking cough, though nothing can cure the condition before it's run its course. Vaccination cannot guarantee protection from canine cough, but it does ward off the most common virus responsible for the condition.

Lyme disease (also called borreliosis), although known for decades, was only first diagnosed in dogs in 1984. Lyme disease can affect cats, cattle, and horses, but especially people. In the U.S., the disease is transmitted by two ticks carrying the *Borrelia burgdorferi* organism: the deer tick (*Ixodes scapularis*) and the western black-legged tick (*Ixodes pacificus*), the latter primarily affects reptiles. In Europe, *Ixodes ricinus* is responsible for spreading Lyme. The disease causes lameness, fever, joint swelling, inappetence, and lethargy. Removal of ticks from the dog's coat can help reduce the chances of Lyme, though not as much as avoiding heavily wooded areas where the dog is most likely to contract ticks. A vaccination is available, though it has not been proven to protect dogs from all strains of the organism that causes the disease.

Rabies is passed to dogs and people through wildlife: in North America, principally through the skunk, fox and raccoon; the bat is not the culprit it was once thought to be. Likewise, the common image of the rabid dog foaming at the mouth with every hair on end is unlikely the truest scenario. A rabid dog exhibits difficulty eating, salivates much and has spells of paralysis and awkwardness. Before a dog reaches this final state, it may experience anxiety, personality changes, irritability and more aggressiveness than is usual. Vaccinations are strongly recommended as rabid dogs are too dangerous to manage and are commonly euthanized. Puppies are generally vaccinated at 12 weeks of age, and then annually. Although rabies is on the decline in the world community, tens of thousands of humans die each

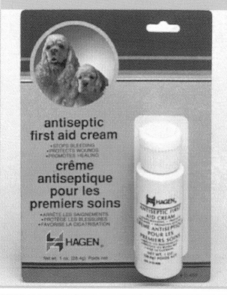

Keep this first aid cream on hand in cases of cuts as it is antiseptic. Photo courtesy of Hagen.

year from rabies-related incidents.

Parasites have clung to our pets for centuries. Despite our modern efforts, fleas still pester our pet's existence, and our own. All dogs itch, and fleas can make even the happiest dog a miserable, scabby mess. The loss of hair and habitual biting and chewing at themselves rank among the annoyances; the nuisances

inside. Discuss the possibilities with your vet. Not all products can be used in conjunction with one another, and some dogs may be more sensitive to certain applications than others. The dog's living quarters must be debugged as well as the dog itself. Heavy infestation may require multiple treatment.

Always check your dog for ticks

Proper maintenance and care are all it takes for a Siberian to live a healthy, happy life.

include the passing of tapeworms and the whole family's itching through the summer months. A full range of flea-control and elimination products are available at pet shops, and your veterinarian surely has recommendations. Sprays, powders, collars and dips fight fleas from the outside; drops and pills fight the good fight from

carefully. Although fleas can be acquired almost anywhere, ticks are more likely to be picked up in heavily treed areas, pastures or other outside grounds (such as dog shows or obedience or field trials). Athletic, active, and hunting dogs are the most likely subjects, though any passing dog can be the host. Remember Lyme disease is passed by tick infestation.

As for internal parasites, worms are potentially dangerous for dogs and people. Roundworms, hookworms, whipworms, tapeworms, and heartworms comprise the blightsome party of troublemakers. Deworming puppies begins at around two to three weeks and continues until three months of age. Proper hygienic care of the environment is also important to prevent contamination with roundworm and hookworm eggs. Heartworm preventatives are recommended by most veterinarians, although there are some drawbacks to the regular introduction of poisons into our dogs' systems.

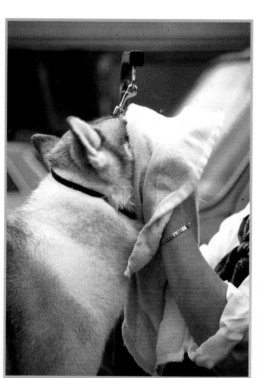

During grooming sessions, carefully clean the dog's face, including his eyes and ears.

These daily or monthly preparations also help regulate most other worms as well. Discuss worming procedures with your veterinarian.

Roundworms pose a great threat to dogs and people. They are found in the intestine of dogs, and can be passed to people through ingestion of feces-contaminated dirt. Roundworm infection can be prevented by not walking dogs in heavy-traffic people areas, by burning feces, and by curbing dogs in a responsible manner. (Of course, in most areas of the country, curbing dogs is the law.) Roundworms are typically passed from the bitch to the litter, and bitches should be treated along with the puppies, even if she tested negative prior to whelping. Generally puppies are treated every two weeks until two months of age.

Hookworms, like roundworms, are also a danger to dogs and people. The hookworm parasite (known as *Ancylostoma caninum*) causes cutaneous larva migrans in people. The eggs of hookworms are passed in feces and become infective in shady, sandy areas. The larvae penetrate the skin of the dog, and the dog subsequently becomes infected. When swallowed, these parasites affect the intestines, lungs, windpipe, and the whole digestive system. Infected dogs suffer from anemia and lose large amounts of blood in the places where the worms latch onto the dog's intestines, etc.

Although infrequently passed to

humans, whipworms are cited as one of the most common parasites in America. These elongated worms affect the intestines of the dog, where they latch on, and cause colic upset or diarrhea. Unless identified in stools passed, whipworms are difficult to diagnose. Adult worms can be eliminated more consistently than the larvae, since whipworms exhibit unusual life cycles. Proper hygienic care of outdoor grounds is critical to the avoidance of these harmful parasites.

dogs do not show great discomfort or symptoms. When people are infected, however, the liver can be seriously damaged. Proper cleanliness is the best bet against tapeworms.

Heartworm disease is transmitted by mosquitoes and badly affects the lungs, heart and blood vessels of dogs. The larvae of *Dirofilaria immitis* enters the dog's bloodstream when bitten by an infected mosquito. The larvae takes about six months to mature. Infected dogs suffer from weight

Ticks, fleas, and other parasites can be just as dangerous to people as they are to dogs. Make sure you thoroughly inspect your Husky's coat for lingering pests during outdoor excursions.

Tapeworms are carried by fleas, and enter the dog when the dog swallows the flea. Humans can acquire tapeworms in the same way, though we are less likely to swallow fleas than dogs are. Recent studies have shown that certain rodents and other wild animals have been infected with tapeworms, and dogs can be affected by catching and/or eating these other animals. Of course, outdoor hunting dogs and terriers are more likely to be infected in this way than are your typical house dog or non-motivated hound. Treatment for tapeworm has proven very effective, and infected

loss, appetite loss, chronic coughing and general fatigue. Not all affected dogs show signs of illness right away, and carrier dogs may be affected for years before clinical signs appear. Treatment of heartworm disease has been effective but can be dangerous also. Prevention as always is the desirable alternative. Ivermectin is the active ingredient in most heartworm preventatives and has proven to be successful. Check with your veterinarian for the preparation best for your dog. Dogs generally begin taking the preventatives at eight months of age and continue to do so throughout the non-winter months.

SUGGESTED READING

The following books are all published by T.F.H. Publications and are recommended to you for additional information:

Successful Dog Training by Michael Kamer (TS-205) contains the latest training methods used by professional dog trainers. Author and Hollywood dog trainer Michael Kamer is one of the most renowned trainers in the country, having trained both stunt dogs for movies and house pets for movie stars such as Frank Sinatra, Barbara Streisand, Arnold Schwarzenegger, Sylvester Stallone, and countless others. The most modern techniques of

SUCCESSFUL DOG TRAINING is one of the better dog training books by Hollywood dog trainer Michael Kamer, who trains dogs for movie stars.

training are presented step-by-step and illustrated with fantastic full-color photography. Whether you are a longtime obedience trainer or a new dog owner, *Successful Dog Training* will prove an invaluable tool in developing or improving your own training skills.

Everybody Can Train Their Own Dog by Angela White (TW-113) is a fabulous reference guide for all dog owners. This well written, easy-to-understand book covers all training topics in alphabetical order for instant location. In addition to teaching, this book provides problem solving and problem prevention techniques that are fundamental to training. All teaching methods are based on motivation and kindness, which bring out the best of a dog's natural ability and instinct.

Owners Guide to Dog Health by Lowell Ackerman, D.V.M. (TS-214) is the most comprehensive volume on dog health available today. Internationally respected veterinarian Dr. Lowell Ackerman examines in full detail the signs of illness and disease, diagnosis, treatment and therapy options as well as preventative measures, all in simple terms that are easy for the reader to understand. Hundreds of color photographs and illustrations throughout the text help explain the latest procedures and technological advances in all areas of canine care, including nutrition, skin and haircoat care, vaccinations, and more. *Owners Guide to Dog Health* is an absolute must for those who sincerely care about the health of their dog.

Dog Breeding for Professionals by Dr. Herbert Richards (H-969) is a straightforward discussion of how to breed dogs of various sizes and how to care for newborn puppies. The many aspects of breeding (including possible problems and practical solutions) are covered in great detail. *Warning: the explicit photos of canine sexual activities may offend some readers.*

The Atlas of Dog Breeds of the World (H-1091) by Bonnie Wilcox, DVM, and Chris Walkowicz traces the history and highlights the characteristics, appearance and function of every recognized dog breed in the world. 409 different

breeds receive full-color treatment and individual study. Hundreds of breeds in addition to those recognized by the American Kennel Club and the Kennel Club of Great Britain are included—the dogs of the world complete! The ultimate reference work, comprehensive coverage, intelligent and delightful discussions. The perfect gift book.

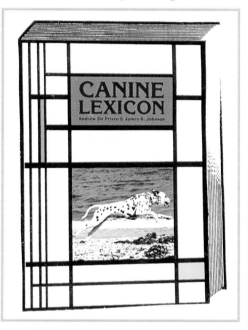

Canine Lexicon by Andrew DePrisco and James Johnson, (TS-175) is an up-to-date encyclopedic dictionary for the dog person. It is the most complete single volume on the dog every published covering more breeds than any other book as well as other relevant topics, including health, showing, training, breeding, anatomy, veterinary terms, and much more. No dog book before has ever offered this many stunning color photographs of all breeds, dog sports, and topics (over 1300 in full color).

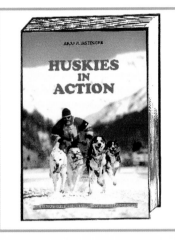

A very successful spinoff of the *Atlas* is *The Mini-Atlas of Dog Breeds*, written by Andrew De Prisco and James B. Johnson. This compact but comprehensive book has been praised and recommended by most national dog publications for its utility and reader-friendliness. The true field guide for dog lovers.

In addition to the foregoing, the following individual dog breed books of interest to readers of this book are available at pet shop and book stores.

Experience the elegance, power, endurance, and sheer joy of sled dog racing in *Huskies in Action*, (TS-234) which offers a close-up look at this awesome sport of man and dog. Author Rico Pfirstinger, who spent three years photographing sled dog races in various parts of Europe, has captured the very essence of the remarkable union between a musher and his dogs. Informatively written and beautifully illustrated with over 120 full-color photographs, *Huskies in Action* chronicles the breathtaking achievements—and

disappointments—of the best sled dog teams in the world.

The Siberian Husky (TS-148) by Joan McDonald Brearley cannot help but attract a greatly diversified audience. New Husky owners and fanciers will find indispensable information on choosing the right puppy, rearing, feeding, breeding and more, while the professional long-time breed lover encounters new, concise material concerning breed development over the past eight decades, accompanied by relevant illustrations, in generous detail.

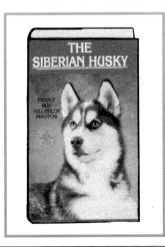